Digital Authority: Strategies for Accounting Firms to Attract Clients with Content

Copyright © 2024 Reginaldo Osnildo
All rights reserved.

PRESENTATION

INTRODUCTION TO CONTENT MARKETING FOR ACCOUNTANTS

DEFINING YOUR TARGET AUDIENCE

PERSONAL BRANDING FOR ACCOUNTANTS

THE POWER OF BLOGGING IN ACCOUNTING

SEO FOR ACCOUNTING WEBSITES

CREATING VALUE CONTENT

SOCIAL MEDIA ENGAGEMENT

VIDEO MARKETING FOR ACCOUNTANTS

EFFECTIVE EMAIL MARKETING FOR ACCOUNTANTS

ONLINE ADVERTISING

DATA ANALYSIS AND METRICS

DIGITAL TOOLS FOR ACCOUNTANTS

ONLINE REPUTATION MANAGEMENT

NETWORKING AND ONLINE PARTNERSHIPS

DIGITAL COMPLIANCE AND ETHICS

WEBINARS AND ONLINE SEMINARS

PRODUCTION OF RICH MATERIALS

COPYWRITING TECHNIQUES FOR ACCOUNTANTS

CONVERSION OPTIMIZATION FOR ACCOUNTING SITES

TARGETED CONTENT STRATEGIES

CUSTOMER FEEDBACK

FUTURE OF DIGITAL MARKETING IN ACCOUNTING

DIGITAL MARKETING CHECKLIST FOR ACCOUNTANTS

30 DAY ACTION PLAN

REGINALDO OSNILDO

PRESENTATION

Welcome to a transformative path where accounting meets the vast and dynamic digital world. This book, **"Digital Authority: Strategies for Accounting Firms to Attract Clients with Content"**, was meticulously crafted with you in mind – the modern accountant looking to not just survive, but thrive in the digital age.

At this point, you may be asking yourself, "Why is this book different?" The answer is simple but powerful. Throughout these pages, I will not only share practical content marketing strategies adjusted to accounting realities, but I will also bring my unique insight to update traditional concepts, making them relevant for today. This book is the result of a careful synthesis of knowledge and experience, designed to facilitate your journey towards digital excellence.

You're about to embark on a journey that ranges from founding an effective digital presence to expanding your online authority through engaging content. This book is your guide to attracting more clients, establishing trust, and positioning yourself as a thought leader in the accounting industry. With practical strategies distributed throughout cohesive and complete chapters, you'll discover how to personalize your brand, optimize your website for search engines, create valuable content, engage on social media, and much more.

With each chapter, you will be invited to explore the next, in a flow that ensures continuity of learning and immediate applicability of the strategies discussed. This book is designed to be your constant companion in the pursuit of digital excellence, providing not only theory but also practical action.

At the end of this journey, you will not only have gained knowledge, but you will also have implemented strategies that will transform the way you operate in the digital world. This is an invitation for you, the accountant, to take a step forward, embrace the changes and become a reference in the online accounting sector.

So, are you ready to start this transformation? Together, let's establish and expand your digital authority, gaining a prominent place in the accounting world. Get ready to enter the first chapter, where we will discuss the " **INTRODUCTION TO CONTENT MARKETING FOR ACCOUNTANTS**" and understand the importance of an effective digital presence. This is just the gateway to the vast universe of possibilities that await you.

Happy reading and a successful journey,

Yours sincerely

Reginaldo Osnildo

INTRODUCTION TO CONTENT MARKETING FOR ACCOUNTANTS

In the accounting world, content marketing emerges as a powerful tool for establishing genuine connections, attracting ideal clients and consolidating your authority in the market. In this chapter, we will explore how you, as an accountant, can use content marketing to create an impactful and effective digital presence. Let's together uncover the importance of a well-designed strategy and how it can transform the way you connect with your target audience.

THE DIGITAL AGE IN ACCOUNTING

The advent of the internet has radically changed the way we communicate, seek information and make decisions. For accounting professionals, this means that the majority of their potential clients are online, browsing for solutions to their accounting questions and needs. Here lies the opportunity: by positioning yourself as a reliable and authoritative source of accounting information, you not only attract customers, but also build a relationship of trust and credibility.

WHAT IS CONTENT MARKETING?

Content marketing is a marketing strategy focused on creating and distributing relevant, valuable, and consistent content to attract and retain a clearly defined audience — and ultimately, to drive profitable customer action. In the context of accounting, this means educating your potential clients on topics such as financial management, taxes, tax planning and much more, using content that answers their questions and needs.

WHY CONTENT MARKETING FOR ACCOUNTANTS?

- **Establishes authority:** Sharing your expert knowledge helps position you as an authority in your field, which is crucial to earning the trust of your clients.

- **Builds relationships:** By providing useful and relevant information, you create a bond with your audience, who begins to see you not just as a service provider, but as a reliable partner.

- **Improves online visibility:** Quality content is also an effective SEO (Search Engine Optimization) tool, helping your website stand out in online searches.

- **Generates qualified leads:** By attracting visitors interested in your content, you increase the chances of converting these visitors into customers.

FIRST STEPS IN CONTENT MARKETING

- **Know your audience:** Before you start producing content, it is essential to understand who your target audience is, what their problems, needs are and how you can help them.

- **Define your goals:** What do you hope to achieve with content marketing? Whether it's increasing brand awareness, generating leads, or establishing authority, having clear goals is crucial.

- **Create valuable content:** Your content must be useful, educational and interesting for your audience. Ask yourself, "Does this add value to my reader?"

- **Promote your content:** Creating content is only half the battle. Use email marketing, social media and other strategies to ensure your content reaches your audience.

As you embark on your content marketing journey, remember that consistency and quality are keys to success. It's not just about publishing content, it's about creating real, lasting connections with your audience.

Now that you understand the importance of content marketing in building your online authority as an accountant, it's time to dive deeper and understand who your target audience really is. In the next chapter, we'll explore techniques for identifying and understanding the specific needs of your ideal customers, ensuring your content is as relevant and impactful as possible.

Ready to take the next step? Let's together uncover the secrets to effectively connecting with your audience and transforming your digital presence.

DEFINING YOUR TARGET AUDIENCE

Deeply understanding who your target audience is represents the foundation upon which all of your content marketing strategies will be built. Without this understanding, even the best-crafted content may not reach its full potential. In this chapter, you'll learn how to identify and understand the specific needs of your ideal customers, creating a genuine, targeted connection that will transform your digital marketing efforts.

THE IMPORTANCE OF KNOWING YOUR TARGET AUDIENCE

First of all, it's crucial to understand why knowing your target audience is so important:

- **Effective communication:** By knowing exactly who you're talking to, you can tailor your language, tone, and message to resonate more deeply with your audience.

- **Relevant content:** By knowing your audience's pains, desires and needs, you can create content that speaks directly to their interests, increasing engagement and retention.

- **Strategic decisions:** With a clear definition of your audience, you can make more informed decisions about which marketing channels to invest in, what type of content to produce and how to optimize your campaigns for better ROI (Return on Investment).

IDENTIFYING YOUR TARGET AUDIENCE

- **Analyze your current customers:** Who are your most valuable customers? What characteristics do they have in common? This information is a valuable starting point.

- **Research the market:** Use market research and online tools to better understand the demographic, psychographic and behavioral characteristics of your ideal audience.

- **Create personas:** Based on the information collected, create detailed "personas", which are semi-fictional representations of your ideal customer. Include details such as age, profession, interests, challenges and goals.

- **Direct feedback:** Don't underestimate the power of direct feedback. Talking to your current or potential customers can reveal valuable insights into their needs and how you can meet them.

UNDERSTANDING YOUR AUDIENCE'S NEEDS

After identifying who your target audience is, the next step is to deeply understand their needs. This can be achieved through:

- **Online behavior analysis:** Tools like Google Analytics can show how visitors interact with your website, which pages they visit most and how they reach you.

- **Keyword research:** Find out what terms your target audience is using in online searches. This may indicate the information they are looking for.

- **Requesting feedback:** Targeted surveys and questionnaires can help gather information about your audience's specific challenges and needs.

APPLYING KNOWLEDGE ABOUT YOUR AUDIENCE

With a clear understanding of your target audience and their needs, you are now in a strong position to:

- **Produce targeted content:** Create content that addresses your audience's specific questions, whether through blog posts, videos, webinars or infographics.

- **Personalize communication:** Adapt your communication to speak directly to your audience, using the channels they prefer, such as email, social networks or podcasts.

- **Develop attractive offers:** Develop services or offers that meet the specific needs of your audience, increasing the chances of conversion.

Now that you understand the importance of defining and knowing your target audience, it's time to delve deeper into how you can highlight your expertise and build a strong personal brand in the next chapter. "**PERSONAL BRANDING FOR ACCOUNTANTS**" will explore how you can position yourself as a thought leader in the accounting industry, utilizing your personal brand to further attract your ideal audience. This is an essential step in establishing trust and credibility, fundamental in the journey to increase your digital authority. Ready to discover how your personal brand can make a difference? Here we go!

PERSONAL BRANDING FOR ACCOUNTANTS

In the world of accounting, where competition is fierce and services often look similar to potential clients, developing a strong personal brand is more than a competitive advantage – it's a necessity. In this chapter, we'll explore how you can build and strengthen your personal brand to highlight your expertise, build trust, and ultimately attract and retain more customers.

THE IMPORTANCE OF PERSONAL BRANDING

Personal branding refers to the practice of promoting yourself and your career as a brand. It's the process of establishing a distinct public image and professional identity that communicates your uniqueness, your values, and the promise of what you offer. For accountants, this means conveying your expertise, trustworthiness, and the unique value you bring to your clients.

STEPS TO BUILDING YOUR PERSONAL BRAND

> 1 - **Define your value proposition:** Identify what differentiates you from others in the accounting field. This may include specific specializations, a unique approach to customer service, or a distinctive business philosophy.
>
> 2 – **Know your target audience:** Building on the previous chapter, use your knowledge of your audience to shape your personal brand in a way that resonates with them.
>
> 3 - **Communicate your story:** Your personal and professional story is a powerful branding tool. Share your journey, challenges overcome and successes achieved in an authentic way.
>
> 4 - **Consistency is key:** Ensure that all your online (website, social media, blog) and offline (networking, business cards) touchpoints communicate your personal brand consistently.
>
> 5 - **Educate and offer value:** Produce content that educates your audience on accounting topics that are important

to them. This establishes your authority and shows your commitment to adding value.

6 - Engage with your community: Participate in events, webinars and forums, both as a spectator and as a speaker. This increases your visibility and reinforces your position as an expert.

7 – Feedback and adjustments: Be open to feedback and be prepared to adjust your personal branding strategy as needed. Personal branding is an ongoing process.

PERSONAL BRAND IN PRACTICE

Let's consider the example of an accountant specializing in technology startups. Your value proposition can be your deep understanding of the specific financial and tax needs of these companies. He can communicate this through a blog with accounting tips for startups, active participation in technology events, and offering free initial consultations to local startups. Each action reinforces your brand as the "counter of tech startups."

THE IMPACT OF PERSONAL BRANDING

Well-executed personal branding can have a significant impact:

- **Differentiation:** In a saturated market, your personal brand can be the differentiator that attracts customers to you instead of a competitor.

- **Trust and credibility:** By consistently demonstrating your expertise, you build trust with your audience, which is essential for converting prospects into customers.

- **Perceived value:** A strong personal brand can allow you to command higher prices for your services, reflecting the greater perceived value you offer.

Now that you understand the importance of personal branding

and how to start building your personal brand, it's time to explore one of the most effective tools for communicating your brand and expertise: blogging. In the next chapter, "**THE POWER OF BLOGGING IN ACCOUNTING**," we'll dive into strategies for creating a successful blog that not only attracts and retains clients, but also strengthens your online presence and authority in the industry. Are you ready to turn your words into a powerful marketing tool? Let's move on!

THE POWER OF BLOGGING IN ACCOUNTING

Blogging is an incredibly powerful tool in the digital marketing arsenal for accountants. It not only serves as a vehicle to share your expertise and knowledge with a wider audience, but it also acts as a magnet to attract potential customers to your website. In this chapter, we'll explore how you can use blogging to create a successful blog that not only attracts and retains clients, but also solidifies your online presence and establishes your authority in the accounting industry.

WHY BLOGGING IS ESSENTIAL FOR ACCOUNTANTS

- **Establishes authority:** Publishing well-researched and informative articles about accounting and finance establishes you as an authority in your field.

- **Improves SEO:** Regular, keyword-rich blogs help improve your website's ranking in search engines, making it easier for potential customers to find you.

- **Builds relationships:** By providing valuable information for free, you build a relationship with your readers, who may become customers.

- **Demonstrates competence:** Discussing complex topics in a clear and accessible way demonstrates your competence and ability to deal with accounting issues.

HOW TO CREATE A SUCCESSFUL BLOG

- **Choose the right topics:** Focus on topics that are not only relevant to your area of expertise, but also of interest to your target audience. This could include industry trends, tax planning tips, guidance for startups, and more.

- **Maintain quality and consistency:** Post content regularly, but don't sacrifice quality for quantity. Well-written, informative and accurate articles are key.

- **Optimize for SEO:** Use relevant keywords, meta descriptions and catchy titles. This not only improves your visibility on search engines but also attracts more readers to your blog.

- **Include calls to action:** Each post should include a call to action, encouraging readers to engage more deeply with your content, whether through comments, shares or newsletter signups.

- **Promote your blog:** Use social media, email marketing and your professional network to promote your posts. Promotion is key to reaching a wider audience.

- **Interact with your readers:** Respond to comments and questions. Interaction not only builds relationships but also encourages loyalty and engagement.

SUCCESSFUL EXAMPLE

Consider the case of an accountant specializing in small businesses. By focusing his blog on common tax and accounting issues faced by small business owners, from simplifying the accounting process to strategies for optimizing taxes, he not only attracts a specific target audience, but also establishes a reputation as the "accounting expert for Small business".

BLOGGING CHALLENGES

- **Maintain consistency:** Producing content regularly can be a challenge, especially for busy professionals.

- **Find relevant topics:** Identifying topics that are of ongoing interest to your audience can require research and insight.

- **Measuring return on investment (ROI):** Assessing the direct impact of blogging on business can be complex, but metrics such as website traffic, engagement and conversions can offer valuable insights.

Now that you understand the power of blogging in accounting, the next chapter will take your digital presence even further by exploring "**SEO FOR ACCOUNTING WEBSITES**." We will learn how to optimize your website and content to ensure you are found by potential clients when they search for accounting services online. Ready to increase your online visibility and attract more customers? Let's dive into the world of SEO.

SEO FOR ACCOUNTING WEBSITES

In today's digital world, being found online by potential clients is more crucial than ever, especially for accountants and accounting professionals. Search engine optimization, or SEO, is the key to improving your online visibility and ensuring that your website is easily found by those looking for the services you offer. This chapter dives into SEO strategies specific to accounting websites, helping you attract more qualified visitors and convert those visitors into customers.

UNDERSTANDING SEO

SEO involves a set of practices designed to improve your website's position in search engine results, such as Google and Bing. This is crucial because most people don't get past the first page of results when searching for services. Therefore, the higher your website ranks, the more likely it is to be found.

SEO STRATEGIES FOR ACCOUNTANTS

- **Keyword research:** Identify the keywords your potential clients are using to find accounting services. Tools like Google Keyword Planner and SEMrush can help. Focus on industry-specific terms as well as long-tail keywords, which are more specific and less competitive.

- **On-page optimization:** Make sure your website is optimized for your chosen keywords. This includes including these keywords in page titles, headers, meta descriptions, and body text. Optimizing images is also important, ensuring they have reduced file sizes and are marked up with relevant alt text.

- **Quality content:** Produce regular and relevant content that answers your target audience's questions and needs. Blogs, articles and case studies not only help improve your search engine rankings but also establish your authority and knowledge in the industry.

- **User experience:** Google values sites that offer a good user experience, including fast page loading, easy navigation, and responsive design that works well on mobile devices.

- Link Building: Get links from other trusted sites to yours. This can be achieved through the creation of shareable content, digital PR and listings in relevant business directories.

- Local SEO: For accountants who primarily serve clients in a specific geographic area, local SEO is essential. This includes optimizing your Google My Business listing and ensuring your contact information is consistent across the web.

MEASURING SUCCESS

Monitoring your website's performance is crucial to understanding the impact of your SEO strategies. Tools like Google Analytics and Google Search Console can provide valuable insights into traffic, keyword rankings, user behavior, and more. Use this information to adjust your strategy as needed.

COMMON CHALLENGES

- Changes in SEO guidelines: Search engines frequently update their algorithms. Staying informed about these changes is crucial to maintaining or improving your rankings.

- SEO is a long-term investment: Significant SEO results can take time. It's an ongoing commitment, not a quick fix.

Now that you have a solid foundation on how to optimize your website for search engines, the next step is to learn how to create content that not only improves your SEO, but also offers real value to your visitors. In the next chapter, " **CREATING VALUE CONTENT**", we will explore strategies for developing content that responds to your clients' questions and needs, further reinforcing your authority and trust in the accounting sector. Ready to take your content to a new level? Let's go.

CREATING VALUE CONTENT

The heart of any effective content marketing strategy, especially in the accounting industry, is the ability to create content that brings genuine value to your customers and target audience. This chapter is dedicated to exploring how you can develop content that not only answers your customers' questions and needs, but also reinforces your authority and credibility in the industry, promoting engagement and loyalty.

WHAT CONSTITUTES VALUE CONTENT?

Valuable content is content that solves problems, answers questions, or offers insights and information that audiences can't easily find elsewhere. In the context of accounting, this could mean anything from in-depth articles on the latest tax changes to step-by-step tutorials on how to improve financial management for small businesses.

STRATEGIES FOR DEVELOPING VALUE CONTENT

- **Understand your audience:** Returning to the chapter on defining your target audience, use this knowledge to create content that speaks directly to their specific concerns, needs and interests.

- **Stay up to date:** In the accounting sector, laws and regulations are constantly changing. Stay up to date and share these updates with your audience in an understandable way.

- **Use real data and examples:** Enrich your content with case studies, real examples and data that clearly demonstrate the points you are discussing. This not only increases the credibility of the content but also makes it more tangible for your audience.

- **Diversified formats:** Vary the formats of your content. In addition to articles and blog posts, consider videos, infographics, podcasts, and webinars. Different formats can suit your audience's different learning and engagement preferences.

- **Interactivity and engagement:** Include quizzes, polls and calls to action that encourage interaction with your content. This can increase engagement and provide valuable feedback about your audience's interests and needs.

- **Optimization for SEO:** When creating valuable content, don't forget to optimize it for search engines, as discussed in the previous chapter. This ensures that your target audience can find your content when they search for relevant topics online.

MEASURING THE IMPACT OF YOUR CONTENT

Evaluating the success of your content is crucial to understanding what resonates with your audience and adjusting your strategy as needed. Use metrics like page views, time spent on site, conversion rates, and social media engagement to measure the impact of your content.

CHALLENGES IN CREATING VALUE CONTENT

- **Consistency and quality:** Maintaining a steady flow of high-quality content can be challenging, especially for accountants with busy schedules.

- **Finding relevant topics:** Continuously identifying new topics that are both current and of interest to your audience requires constant research and insight.

- **Measure ROI:** While essential, it can be difficult to directly attribute new business or customers to your content effort, making calculating return on investment a complex task.

With a solid understanding of how to create valuable content, the next step is to learn how to promote it and engage with your audience on the platforms where they spend time: social media. In the next chapter, "**SOCIAL MEDIA ENGAGEMENT**," we'll explore how to use these platforms to connect with your audience, promote your content, and reinforce your brand and online authority. Are you ready to expand your reach and engagement? Let's move forward.

SOCIAL MEDIA ENGAGEMENT

Social media is a vital extension of the digital space where accountants can broaden their reach, engage directly with audiences and promote their valuable content. This chapter is designed to explore effective strategies for utilizing social media platforms to not only connect with your audience, but also to strengthen your personal brand and authority in the accounting industry.

THE IMPORTANCE OF SOCIAL MEDIA FOR ACCOUNTANTS

On social media, you have the opportunity to show a more personal side of your brand, making it more accessible and trustworthy. These platforms allow you to:

- **Communicate directly:** With your audience by answering questions, offering advice and receiving feedback.

- **Promote your content:** Sharing your articles, videos and insights to drive traffic back to your website.

- **Build community:** Creating a space for relevant discussions, mutual support and knowledge sharing.

EFFECTIVE STRATEGIES FOR ENGAGEMENT ON SOCIAL MEDIA

- **Choose the right platforms:** It is not necessary to be on all platforms. Choose the ones where your target audience is most active. For many accountants, LinkedIn, Twitter and Facebook are common choices.

- **Create a content calendar:** Plan your posts in advance. This helps maintain a consistent presence and ensure you are covering a variety of relevant topics.

- **Interact with your audience:** Respond to comments, questions and messages. Interaction shows that you value your community and helps build stronger relationships.

- **Use visual content:** Images, infographics and videos tend to perform better on social media. They can help explain complex accounting concepts in a more accessible way.

- **Drive engagement:** Ask questions, create polls, and invite your audience to share their own experiences. This can increase interactivity and engagement.

- **Monitor and adjust:** Use the analytics tools offered by social media platforms to monitor the performance of your posts. Adjust your strategy based on what works best.

EXAMPLE OF SUCCESSFUL ENGAGEMENT

Imagine an accountant who specializes in services for freelancers and self-employed professionals. He uses LinkedIn to share weekly tips on financial management and tax preparation, while on Instagram, he posts visual infographics simplifying new tax laws. By actively responding to questions and comments, he builds an engaged and informed community.

CHALLENGES OF ENGAGEMENT IN SOCIAL MEDIA

- **Maintain consistency:** Posting regularly and interacting with the public can be challenging, especially for professionals with busy schedules.

- **Appropriate content:** Finding the right balance between being professional and personal can be tricky, but it's crucial to building an authentic and trustworthy brand.

- **Measuring ROI:** Determining the exact return on investment in social media can be difficult, but the focus should be on building long-term relationships and authority.

With social media engagement strategies well underway, the next step is to explore one of the most effective forms of digital content: video. In the next chapter, "**VIDEO MARKETING FOR ACCOUNTANTS**", we'll discuss how you can use videos to educate, engage and convert your target audience, leveraging the power of visual storytelling to further strengthen your online presence.

Ready to bring your brand to life through video? Let's proceed.

VIDEO MARKETING FOR ACCOUNTANTS

Video has emerged as one of the most engaging and effective forms of content in the digital age, offering a powerful way to communicate complexities, share insights, and establish a personal connection with your audience. For accountants and accounting professionals, incorporating video marketing into your communication strategy can be a differentiator, helping to educate, engage and convert your audience more effectively. In this chapter, we'll explore how you can use video marketing to highlight your expertise, value, and your brand's unique personality.

WHY VIDEO?

- **High engagement:** Videos have the ability to capture audience attention more effectively than texts or static images.

- **Complexity made simple:** Explain complicated accounting concepts clearly and easily through visual explanations.

- **Personal connection:** Videos allow you to convey your personality and build trust by "humanizing" your brand.

- **SEO-Friendly:** Videos can improve your website's SEO, especially when shared on YouTube, which is owned by Google.

HOW TO USE VIDEOS EFFECTIVELY

- **Define your purpose:** Each video should have a clear purpose, whether that's educating about a specific topic, sharing industry news, or promoting a service.

- **Keep it accessible:** Short, to-the-point videos tend to work best. Try to keep most of your videos between 2 to 5 minutes.

- **Focus on quality:** Invest in good lighting, clear audio, and professional editing to ensure your videos look and sound high quality.

- **Include a call to action:** Encourage viewers to engage more deeply with your brand, whether by subscribing to your channel, visiting your website, or getting in touch for more information.

- **Diversify formats:** Try different types of videos, such as tutorials, Q&As, customer testimonials, and service overviews.

- **Promote your videos:** Share your videos on your website, social media and newsletters to reach a wider audience.

VIDEO EXAMPLES FOR ACCOUNTANTS

- **Step-by-step tutorials:** Ideal for explaining complex accounting processes or accounting software.

- **Legislative updates:** Share changes in tax laws and how they affect your clients.

- **Financial advice:** Offer tips on financial management and tax planning.

- **Customer success stories:** Testimonials from satisfied customers that highlight how your service made a difference.

VIDEO MARKETING CHALLENGES

- **Required resources:** Video production can require more time and financial resources than other types of content.

- **Technical barrier:** Learning video recording and editing skills can present a learning curve for beginners.

- **Visibility and engagement:** As with any content, ensuring your videos are seen and engage your audience is a constant challenge.

Now that we've explored how video marketing can be a valuable tool for building your online presence and engaging your audience, the next step is to look at one of the oldest but still incredibly effective digital marketing strategies: email marketing. In the next chapter, **"EFFECTIVE EMAIL MARKETING FOR ACCOUNTANTS"**, we'll discuss how to use email to maintain a direct and valuable communication channel with your customer base, from capturing new leads to building loyalty with existing customers. Ready to maximize your reach and impact through email? Let's go ahead.

EFFECTIVE EMAIL MARKETING FOR ACCOUNTANTS

Email marketing remains one of the most powerful and cost-effective tools for accountants and accounting professionals looking to maintain direct, meaningful communication with their client base. In this chapter, we'll explore how you can use email marketing to not only capture new leads, but also to nurture and retain your existing customers by offering valuable, personalized content.

WHY EMAIL MARKETING?

- **Direct customer access:** Email allows you to deliver your message directly to your customer's inbox, without the distraction and volatility of social media.

- **Cost-effective:** Compared to other forms of digital marketing, email marketing offers one of the best returns on investment (ROI).

- **Personalization:** Emails can be highly personalized, from audience segmentation to personalizing messages based on user behavior.

- **Measurement of results:** Email marketing tools offer detailed analyzes on opens, clicks and conversions, allowing strategic adjustments.

STRATEGIES FOR EFFECTIVE EMAIL MARKETING

- **Build your email list:** Never buy email lists. Instead, build yours organically by encouraging sign-ups through your website, blog and social media.

- **Audience segmentation:** Divide your email list based on criteria such as type of service of interest, location or stage in the purchasing cycle to personalize messages more effectively.

- **Provide valuable content:** Send regular newsletters with industry updates, accounting tips, important deadline reminders, and exclusive access to new resources.

- **Responsive design:** Make sure your emails are visually appealing and easy to read on mobile devices, where most people access their electronic correspondence.

- **Clear calls to action:** Include clear and compelling calls to action (CTAs), encouraging readers to take the next step, whether that's scheduling an appointment, downloading a free resource, or reading the latest blog post.

- **Automated follow-up:** Use automated email sequences to nurture leads over time, especially after they download a resource or register for a webinar.

EXAMPLES OF EMAIL CAMPAIGNS FOR ACCOUNTANTS

- **Monthly newsletters:** Keep your clients and leads informed about the latest accounting industry news and insights.

- **Educational Email Series:** Create an email series covering fundamental accounting topics for small businesses, freelancers, or startups, depending on your target audience.

- **End of tax year reminders:** Send personalized reminders about important deadlines and tax planning tips.

EMAIL MARKETING CHALLENGES

- **Email overload:** Many people receive a large amount of emails daily, so making yours stand out is essential.

- **List maintenance:** Maintaining a clean and engaged email list requires ongoing effort, including removing inactive subscribers and adjusting targeting.

- **Relevant content:** Creating content that is both relevant and engaging for different segments of your audience can be challenging, but it is crucial to the success of campaigns.

With the foundations of email marketing established, it's time to explore another vital component of your digital marketing strategy: online advertising. In the next chapter, "**ONLINE ADVERTISING**", we will discuss how you can use paid advertising to reach a larger, more targeted audience, maximizing your visibility and attracting potential customers. Ready to amplify your reach with online ads? Let's dive into this strategy.

ONLINE ADVERTISING

In an increasingly saturated digital world, standing out and reaching your specific target audience requires not only organic strategies but also the smart use of online ads. For accountants and accounting professionals, paid advertising can be an effective way to reach a larger, more targeted audience, driving qualified traffic to your website or specific offers. In this chapter, we'll explore how you can make the most of online ads to grow your digital presence and attract more potential customers.

THE IMPORTANCE OF ONLINE ADVERTISING FOR ACCOUNTANTS

- **Targeted Reach:** Online ads allow you to reach specific people based on criteria such as location, interests, online behavior and more, increasing the chances of reaching those who are actively looking for accounting services.

- **Measurable results:** With online ads, you can easily track the performance of your campaigns in real time, adjusting your strategies to maximize your return on investment (ROI).

- **Budget flexibility:** You can start with any budget, adjusting it as needed to optimize results. This makes online advertising affordable even for small accounting firms or independent accountants.

EFFECTIVE STRATEGIES FOR ONLINE ADVERTISING

- **Google Ads:** Take advantage of paid search to appear in search results when potential clients are looking for specific accounting services. Use keywords that are relevant to your target audience and your offer.

- **Facebook and Instagram Ads:** These platforms offer robust targeting options, allowing you to target your ads to the exact audience you want to reach, based on demographics, interests and behaviors.

- **LinkedIn Ads:** For accountants focused on corporate or B2B services, LinkedIn can be a valuable platform for ads, allowing you to reach decision-makers and professionals in specific industries.

- **Remarketing:** Use remarketing to reach people who visited your website but didn't take a desired action, like scheduling an appointment or signing up for your newsletter. This helps keep your brand in the minds of potential customers.

- **Create optimized landing pages:** For each ad campaign, create a specific landing page that matches the ad's message and encourages a clear action, whether it's filling out a contact form, downloading a free resource, or scheduling an appointment.

MEASURING THE SUCCESS OF YOUR ONLINE ADS

Use analytics tools to track the performance of your ads, including clicks, conversions, cost per acquisition (CPA), and return on investment (ROI). Adjust your campaigns based on this data to continually improve your results.

CHALLENGES OF ONLINE ADVERTISING

- **High competition:** Depending on your niche, you may face high competition for keywords and audiences, which can increase the cost of ads.

- **Maintain relevance:** Ensuring your ads are relevant and valuable to your target audience requires continuous testing and optimization.

With a solid understanding of how online ads can be used to expand your reach, the next step is to dive into data analysis and metrics. In the next chapter, we'll explore how to measure the success of your digital marketing strategies, including your online advertising, to continually optimize your efforts and ensure the best return on investment. This knowledge will allow you to make data-driven decisions, adjusting your strategies to achieve maximum success. Ready to turn data into actionable insights? Let's go.

DATA ANALYSIS AND METRICS

Data and metrics analysis is critical to understanding the success of your digital marketing strategies, including online ads, email marketing, SEO and social media engagement. This chapter focuses on how you, as an accountant or accounting professional, can use data and metrics to evaluate the effectiveness of your campaigns, optimize your strategies and ensure maximum return on investment (ROI).

THE IMPORTANCE OF DATA ANALYSIS IN DIGITAL MARKETING

- **Data-driven decision making:** Using real data to inform your marketing strategies can significantly increase the effectiveness of your campaigns.

- **Identification of trends and patterns:** Data analysis helps identify what works (and what doesn't), allowing for strategic adjustments that better align with your audience's preferences.

- **Measuring ROI:** Understanding which tactics deliver the best return helps you allocate resources more efficiently, maximizing your marketing budget.

CRUCIAL METRICS TO MONITOR

- **Website traffic:** The amount of traffic and the sources of that traffic (organic, paid, direct, referrals) offer valuable insights into the effectiveness of your SEO and online advertising strategies.

- **Conversion rate:** The percentage of visitors who take the desired action (such as filling out a contact form or downloading a guide) helps you evaluate the effectiveness of your landing pages and calls to action.

- **Cost per acquisition (CPA):** How much does it cost to acquire a new customer through your marketing campaigns? This metric is vital to understanding the sustainability of your paid advertising strategies.

- **Engagement on social media:** Metrics such as likes, shares, comments and follower growth rate can indicate the level of engagement and interest of your audience.

- **Email open and click rates (CTRs):** The open rate and CTR of your emails indicate how relevant and engaging your audience finds the content you send.

ANALYSIS AND MONITORING TOOLS

- **Google Analytics:** Provides a comprehensive view of user behavior on your website, including traffic, traffic sources, and conversions.

- **Google Search Console:** Helps monitor your website's visibility in Google search results, in addition to identifying technical problems.

- **Email marketing tools:** Platforms like Mailchimp and Constant Contact offer detailed analysis on the performance of your emails.

- **Social media management tools:** Tools like Hootsuite and Buffer allow you to monitor engagement on social media and analyze the performance of your posts.

HOW TO USE DATA TO OPTIMIZE STRATEGIES

- **A/B testing:** Use A/B testing on emails, landing pages and ads to determine which versions generate better performance.

- **Ad targeting adjustment:** Based on ad performance, adjust targeting to better reach your target audience.

- **Personalized content:** Use demographic and behavioral data to personalize the content of emails and offers, increasing relevance and conversion rate.

- **SEO and keywords:** Adjust your content and SEO strategy based on the keywords that drive the most traffic and conversions.

CHALLENGES IN DATA ANALYSIS

- **Information overload:** With so many metrics available, it can be challenging to identify which are the most important to focus on.

- **Data interpretation:** Understanding what data really means and how to act based on it requires a certain skill and experience.

Armed with a solid understanding of how to analyze and utilize data to optimize your digital marketing strategies, the next step is to explore digital tools that can facilitate and amplify your marketing efforts and daily operations. In the next chapter, "**DIGITAL TOOLS FOR ACCOUNTANTS**," we'll dive into technologies and software that can help streamline processes, improve efficiency, and boost customer engagement. Ready to discover the tools that will transform your business? Let's move on.

DIGITAL TOOLS FOR ACCOUNTANTS

As accounting and digital marketing become increasingly intertwined, effective use of digital tools becomes essential for accountants and accounting professionals. These tools not only simplify operational and marketing processes, they also improve efficiency, increase customer engagement and drive business growth. In this chapter, we'll explore a selection of technologies and software that can transform your accounting practice, from customer relationship management (CRM) to marketing automation and financial analysis tools.

CRM (CUSTOMER RELATIONSHIP MANAGEMENT)

- **Salesforce:** Offers a comprehensive CRM solution that can be customized to the needs of any accounting firm, making it easier to manage leads, customers and sales opportunities.

- **HubSpot:** In addition to its powerful CRM capabilities, HubSpot provides integrated marketing and sales tools, making it ideal for accountants looking for a unified marketing approach.

MARKETING AUTOMATION

- **Mailchimp:** Allows the creation, sending and analysis of email marketing campaigns. Its automation features save time by sending personalized emails to specific segments of your list.

- **ActiveCampaign :** Combines email marketing, automation, automated sales and CRM. It's particularly useful for creating automated sales funnels and precisely segmenting contacts.

FINANCIAL ANALYSIS TOOLS

- **QuickBooks :** Widely used by accountants, QuickBooks makes accounting easy, from payroll to cash flow management and tax preparation.

- **Xero:** An alternative to QuickBooks , Xero is loved for its user-friendly interface, automation of accounting tasks, and integration with a wide range of third-party applications.

PROJECT MANAGEMENT AND COLLABORATION

- **Asana** : A project management tool that helps accounting teams organize, track, and manage their work, from daily tasks to long-term projects.

- **Slack:** Facilitates internal communication, allowing teams to share files, organize conversations by topic and integrate third-party tools for a more efficient workflow.

CLOUD SECURITY AND STORAGE

- **Dropbox Business:** Provides secure cloud storage and file sharing solutions, ensuring important documents are always accessible and protected.

- **LastPass** : A password manager that ensures that all your digital tool accounts are protected by strong and unique passwords, minimizing the risk of security breaches.

CHALLENGES WHEN IMPLEMENTING DIGITAL TOOLS

- **Learning curve:** Adopting new technologies may require time for training and adaptation by the team.

- **Systems integration:** Ensuring that new tools integrate effectively with existing systems can be a technical challenge.

- **Cost:** While many tools offer excellent ROI, the initial cost and ongoing subscriptions need to be factored into the budget.

With an arsenal of digital tools at your disposal to optimize your operations and marketing strategies, the next step is to ensure your online reputation lives up to your quality service offering. In the next chapter, **"ONLINE REPUTATION MANAGEMENT"**, we will discuss strategies for monitoring and improving your digital presence, building trust and credibility with your target audience. Ready to strengthen your online reputation? Let's move forward.

ONLINE REPUTATION MANAGEMENT

Online reputation has become a crucial component of success in the digital world for accountants and accounting professionals. A positive reputation builds trust and credibility, two essential elements for attracting and retaining customers. This chapter will cover how to monitor your digital presence, manage customer feedback, and implement strategies to improve your online reputation.

DIGITAL PRESENCE MONITORING

- **Google Alerts:** Set up alerts for your business name, services, and related keywords to monitor online mentions and promptly respond to any concerns or negative feedback.

- **Social media monitoring tools:** Use tools like Hootsuite or Buffer to monitor what is being said about your brand on social media and proactively engage with your audience.

CUSTOMER FEEDBACK MANAGEMENT

- **Request reviews:** Encourage satisfied customers to leave positive reviews on platforms like Google My Business and social media. Positive reviews increase your visibility and credibility.

- **Respond to all reviews:** Be prompt and professional when responding to reviews, both positive and negative. Demonstrate that you value feedback and are willing to make improvements if necessary.

- **Manage criticism constructively:** In the case of negative feedback, address the issue calmly and offer a solution. This can turn a negative experience into an opportunity to demonstrate your commitment to customer satisfaction.

STRATEGIES TO IMPROVE ONLINE REPUTATION

- **Quality content:** Continue to produce and share valuable and educational content. This not only improves your SEO but also establishes your authority and trustworthiness in the accounting field.

- **Active presence on social media:** An active and positive presence on social media can significantly improve your online reputation. Share successes, customer stories and participate in relevant discussions.

- **Partnerships and collaborations:** Collaborate with other respected brands and industry professionals to broaden your network and improve your visibility and reputation.

- **Transparency:** Be transparent about your services, prices and processes. Clarity helps build trust with your customers and the general public.

CHALLENGES OF ONLINE REPUTATION MANAGEMENT

- **Crisis management:** Knowing how to deal with online reputation crises quickly and effectively is crucial, but can be challenging without the right strategy.

- **Ongoing maintenance:** Online reputation management is not a "set it and forget it" thing - it requires constant monitoring and engagement.

- **Balance between personal and professional:** Finding the right balance in your online presence, remaining professional but approachable and human, can be tricky.

With your online reputation solidified, the next step is to further expand your network of professional contacts through online networking and partnerships. In the next chapter, **"NETWORKING AND ONLINE PARTNERSHIPS,"** we'll explore how you can use digital platforms to connect with other professionals, establish strategic partnerships, and expand your reach and influence in the accounting industry. Are you ready to take your professional network to the next level? Let's proceed.

NETWORKING AND ONLINE PARTNERSHIPS

In the dynamic accounting world, developing a robust network of professional contacts and establishing strategic partnerships can mean the difference between success and stagnation. The internet offers an unparalleled platform to expand your network and build valuable professional relationships. In this chapter, we'll explore how to use online networking and partnerships to expand your reach, strengthen your brand, and open up new business opportunities.

WHY ONLINE NETWORKING IS ESSENTIAL

- **Expanded access:** The internet breaks down geographic barriers, allowing you to connect with professionals and potential clients around the world.

- **Increased visibility:** By actively participating in online discussions and collaborating with other professionals, you increase the visibility of your personal and business brand.

- **Learning opportunities:** Networking online also offers the chance to learn from peers, stay up to date on industry trends, and acquire new skills.

STRATEGIES FOR EFFECTIVE ONLINE NETWORKING AND PARTNERSHIPS

- **LinkedIn:** Keep your profile updated and be active on the platform, participating in industry groups, sharing relevant content and connecting with other professionals. LinkedIn is also an excellent place to identify and initiate strategic partnerships.

- **Webinars and virtual events:** Participating in and, when possible, presenting webinars and virtual events are powerful ways to demonstrate your expertise while expanding your network.

- **Content collaborations:** Working together with other professionals to create content (blogs, videos, podcasts) not only strengthens your relationships, but also doubles the reach of your message.

- **Social media:** In addition to LinkedIn, use other social media platforms to engage with the accounting community, share insights, and collaborate on projects or discussions.

- **Professional Forums:** Participating in industry-specific online forums and communities can be a valuable way to establish connections with colleagues who share similar interests and challenges.

BENEFITS OF ONLINE PARTNERSHIPS

- **Resource sharing:** Partnerships can offer access to complementary resources and knowledge, benefiting both parties.

- **New markets:** Collaborating with partners can open doors to new markets and customer segments that would be difficult to reach alone.

- **Brand strengthening:** Association with other respected and professional brands can reinforce your credibility and authority in the sector.

CHALLENGES OF NETWORKING AND ONLINE PARTNERSHIPS

- **Building authentic relationships:** Developing genuine, long-term relationships online can take time and requires effective and consistent communication.

- **Partner selection:** Identifying and choosing the right partners requires diligence and alignment of values and objectives.

After strengthening your professional network and establishing strategic partnerships, it is crucial to carefully navigate the waters of compliance and digital ethics. In the next chapter, "**DIGITAL COMPLIANCE AND ETHICS**", we will discuss best practices to ensure your online activities comply with relevant regulations and maintain the highest ethical standards. This knowledge is essential to protect your reputation and the trust of your customers. Ready to delve deeper into compliance and digital ethics? We will move forward together.

DIGITAL COMPLIANCE AND ETHICS

Navigating the online environment requires not only skill and knowledge, but also a firm commitment to compliance and digital ethics. For accountants and accounting professionals, who operate in a highly regulated and trust-based industry, adhering to these principles is critical. This chapter covers best practices for ensuring your online activities comply with applicable regulations and uphold the highest ethical standards.

UNDERSTANDING COMPLIANCE AND DIGITAL ETHICS

- **Digital compliance:** Refers to compliance with laws, regulations and guidelines that govern online presence and activities. This includes data protection, user privacy and financial regulations specific to the accounting industry.

- **Digital ethics:** It involves conducting your online activities in an ethical manner, respecting the rights and dignity of others, ensuring the authenticity and accuracy of shared information and maintaining the confidentiality of customer data.

PRINCIPLES OF COMPLIANCE AND DIGITAL ETHICS

- **Data protection and privacy:** Ensure that your website's privacy policies are up to date and in compliance with laws such as GDPR in Europe and LGPD in Brazil. Implement robust security measures to protect customer data.

- **Transparency and authenticity:** Be transparent about your services, fees and processes. Ensure all information shared online is accurate and verifiable.

- **Confidentiality:** Maintain the confidentiality of customer information, using only secure platforms for communication and data storage.

- **Respect copyright:** Only use content (images, text, videos) for which you have permission or that is copyright-free, and give appropriate credit when using the work of others.

IMPLEMENTING COMPLIANCE AND DIGITAL ETHICS

- **Continuing education:** Stay informed on the latest privacy and data security laws, as well as ethical best practices for your online presence.

- **Regular audits:** Conduct regular audits of your online presence and data handling practices to identify and correct potential vulnerabilities or non-compliances.

- **Clear policies:** Develop and implement clear data use and privacy policies, both internally and for your customers, and ensure everyone in your organization is aware of and trained on these policies.

- **Tools and technology:** Invest in cutting-edge security technology to protect customer data and utilize consent management tools to ensure compliance with privacy regulations.

CHALLENGES OF COMPLIANCE AND DIGITAL ETHICS

- **Regulatory complexity:** The regulatory landscape for data protection and online privacy is constantly evolving, making compliance a moving target.

- **Cybersecurity risks:** As technologies advance, so do the techniques of cybercriminals, posing an ongoing challenge to data security.

With the foundations of digital compliance and ethics established, the next step is to use webinars and online seminars as tools to educate, engage and expand your customer base. In the next chapter, "**WEBINARS AND ONLINE SEMINARS**," we'll explore how to plan, promote, and execute effective online events that can reinforce your industry authority and boost your business. Ready to capture your target audience's attention through webinars? Let's move forward.

WEBINARS AND ONLINE SEMINARS

Webinars and online seminars have become indispensable tools for accountants and accounting professionals looking to educate, engage and expand their client base in the digital environment. They offer an effective way to share knowledge, demonstrate expertise and interact directly with your target audience, all with a global reach. In this chapter, we'll explore the steps to plan, promote, and execute successful webinars and online seminars.

PLANNING YOUR WEBINAR OR ONLINE SEMINAR

- **Define your goal:** Whether it's educating about a new tax regulation, demonstrating an accounting service, or simply engaging with your community, having a clear goal is essential.

- **Choose the right topic:** The topic must be relevant and of interest to your target audience. Consider frequently asked customer questions for inspiration.

- **Selecting the platform:** Choose a webinar platform that meets your needs, considering number of participants, interaction tools and recording features.

- **Prepare your content:** Develop an attractive and informative presentation. Include data, case studies, and practical examples to make your webinar more valuable.

PROMOTING YOUR WEBINAR

- **Utilize your channels:** Promote your webinar on your website, email, social media and other digital marketing channels.

- **Early registration:** Encourage early registration by offering bonus materials or discounts on services to participants.

- **Partnerships:** Consider collaborating with other professionals or organizations to reach a wider audience.

RUNNING YOUR WEBINAR

- **Technical test:** Do a technical test before the event to ensure everything works smoothly, from audio and video to screen sharing.

- **Interact with the audience:** Use polls, Q&A sessions, and live chat to make the webinar interactive and engaging.

- **Feedback and follow-up:** After the event, send a thank you email to attendees with a link to the webinar recording and request feedback to improve future events.

BENEFITS OF WEBINARS AND ONLINE SEMINARS

- **Establishing authority:** Sharing your knowledge on complex accounting topics can solidify your reputation as an expert in the field.

- **Lead generation:** Webinars provide an opportunity to capture contact information from attendees interested in your services.

- **Cost-effectiveness:** Compared to in-person events, webinars are relatively low cost and can have a much wider reach.

WEBINARS AND ONLINE SEMINAR CHALLENGES

- **Audience engagement:** Keeping your audience engaged virtually, especially in longer sessions, can be challenging.

- **Technical issues:** Technical issues may arise during the event, so it is crucial to have a plan B in case of connection or audio failures.

After mastering the art of running successful webinars and online seminars, the next step is to delve into the production of rich materials such as e- books, guides and infographics. In the next chapter, " **PRODUCTION OF RICH MATERIALS**", we will discuss how these resources can be used to attract and convert leads, further strengthening your authority in the market. Are you ready to create content that captivates and converts? Let's move forward.

PRODUCTION OF RICH MATERIALS

The production of rich materials, such as e-books, guides and infographics, is an effective strategy for attracting and converting leads, as well as reinforcing your authority and presence in the accounting sector. These resources offer significant added value to your potential customers, educating them on important topics while positioning your brand as a trusted source of information. In this chapter, we'll explore how you can develop and utilize rich materials to maximize your digital marketing impact.

BENEFITS OF RICH MATERIALS

- **Lead generation:** By offering rich materials like free downloads, you can capture valuable contact information from interested leads.

- **Customer education:** Provide an opportunity to educate your audience about industry complexities in an accessible and understandable way.

- **Brand reinforcement:** Well-produced and informative materials help strengthen your brand, reinforcing your reputation as an expert on the subject.

PLANNING YOUR RICH MATERIALS

- **Identify your audience's needs:** Choose topics that resonate with your target audience, based on frequently asked questions, common challenges, or emerging themes in the accounting industry.

- **Decide the format:** Depending on your audience and content, choose the most suitable format. E-books and guides are great for in-depth topic explorations, while infographics are ideal for presenting data in a visually appealing way.

- **Content production:** Content must be clear, concise and well organized. Use eye-catching design and keep your brand consistent in terms of style and tone.

DISTRIBUTION AND PROMOTION

- **Landing pages:** Create specific landing pages for each rich material, highlighting the main benefits and including a simple form for capturing leads.

- **Email marketing:** Use your email list to promote your rich materials directly to your contacts, encouraging them to download or sign up.

- **Social media and paid ads:** Promote your materials on social media and consider using paid ads to reach a wider audience.

MEASURING SUCCESS

- **Downloads and leads generated:** Monitor how many people download your materials and how many leads are generated from these actions.

- **Engagement and feedback:** Analyze social media engagement, comments and direct feedback to gauge reception from your audience.

- **Conversion analysis:** Track how many of the leads captured through rich materials convert into paying customers.

CHALLENGES IN THE PRODUCTION OF RICH MATERIALS

- **Resources required:** Producing high-quality materials can be resource-intensive, both in terms of time and budget.

- **Maintaining relevance:** The accounting industry is always changing, so it's vital to update your materials to ensure they remain relevant and accurate.

Now that you're equipped with the knowledge to produce rich materials that educate, engage and convert, the next step is to hone your copywriting skills. In the next chapter,

" **COPYWRITING TECHNIQUES FOR ACCOUNTANTS**," we'll focus on how to write persuasive copy that captures your audience's attention, communicates the value of your services, and encourages action. Mastering copywriting is essential to maximizing the impact of all your marketing materials, from your website homepage to your emails and social media posts. Ready to write in a way that converts more leads into customers? Let's move forward.

COPYWRITING TECHNIQUES FOR ACCOUNTANTS

Mastering the art of copywriting is crucial for accountants and accounting professionals who want to effectively communicate the value of their services, engage their target audience, and convert leads into customers. Persuasive text can make all the difference, whether in your website content, in email marketing campaigns or in social media posts. In this chapter, we'll explore key copywriting techniques that can help enhance your messages and maximize their impact.

UNDERSTANDING THE POWER OF COPYWRITING

- **Clear and concise communication:** In the world of accounting, where concepts can be complex, it is vital that your communication is clear and direct, avoiding jargon that could confuse readers.

- **Focus on benefit:** Your texts should always emphasize the benefits of your services for customers, answering the essential question: "What's in it for me?"

- **Effective calls to action:** Each piece of copy should include a clear call to action (CTA), encouraging the reader to take the next step, whether that's scheduling an appointment, downloading a guide, or signing up for a newsletter.

COPYWRITING TECHNIQUES FOR ACCOUNTANTS

- **AIDA (Attention, Interest, Desire, Action):** Use this classic marketing framework to guide the reader through a journey, from capturing their attention to encouraging them to take action.

- **Personalization:** Use data and insights about your target audience to personalize your message, making it more relevant and attractive to specific customer segments.

- **Social proof:** Include customer testimonials, case studies, and reviews to build credibility and trust in your services.

- **Benefits rather than features:** Emphasize how your

services can solve problems or improve the customer's situation, rather than simply listing the features of your services.

- **Use strong hooks:** Start with powerful openings that spark curiosity or present a key benefit, to ensure readers want to keep reading.

- **Positive language:** Focusing on positive language can help create a sense of optimism and possibility, especially important in communications related to finance and accounting.

APPLYING COPYWRITING IN DIFFERENT CHANNELS

- **Website:** Your website is often the first point of contact with potential customers. Make sure the copy on your home, about us, and services pages clearly communicates your value.

- **Email marketing:** Personalize your emails for different segments of your list, keeping messages focused and direct, with clear CTAs.

- **Social media:** Adapt your writing style to each platform, keeping the text brief and attractive, with a strong focus on engagement.

CHALLENGES OF COPYWRITING IN ACCOUNTING

- **Balancing professionalism and approachability:** Finding the right tone that is professional, yet approachable and engaging, can be a challenge.

- **Stay up to date:** The accounting industry is always changing, requiring your copy to reflect the latest trends and regulations.

Now that you understand how to write persuasive copy, the next step is to focus on optimizing your website for conversion. In the next chapter, "**CONVERSION OPTIMIZATION FOR ACCOUNTING WEBSITES**," we'll cover strategies to ensure your website not only attracts visitors but also converts them into customers. These techniques will help you improve website usability, enhance the customer journey, and maximize your conversion rates. Ready to turn your website into a conversion machine? Let's move forward.

CONVERSION OPTIMIZATION FOR ACCOUNTING SITES

Conversion optimization is essential for turning your website traffic into actual customers. For accountants and accounting professionals, an optimized website can mean the difference between a prospect who browses and leaves and one who takes the desired action, like scheduling an appointment or signing up for a newsletter. In this chapter, we will explore effective strategies to improve your website's usability, enhance the user journey and, consequently, increase your conversion rates.

UNDERSTANDING CONVERSION OPTIMIZATION

Conversion optimization (CRO) involves making adjustments to your website's design and content to increase the percentage of visitors who take a specific action. This can range from filling out a contact form to making a purchase (in the case of digital products or online courses offered by accountants).

EFFECTIVE CRO STRATEGIES FOR ACCOUNTANTS

- **Website traffic analysis:** Use tools like Google Analytics to understand how visitors interact with your website. Identify pages with high traffic but low conversion rates as starting points for optimization.

- **Responsive design:** Ensure your website offers a fluid and intuitive user experience on all devices, especially smartphones and tablets.

- **Clear calls to action:** Every page on your website should have a clear and visible call to action (CTA), encouraging visitors to take the next step in the customer journey.

- **Simplified forms:** Reduce the number of fields on contact or registration forms to the minimum necessary, making the conversion process as easy as possible for visitors.

- **Social proof:** Include testimonials, reviews and case studies from satisfied customers to build trust and encourage new visitors to convert.

- **Website speed:** Optimize the loading speed of your website pages, as slowness can negatively affect conversion rates.

- **A/B Testing:** Perform A/B tests on key elements of your website, such as CTAs, headlines and images, to determine which versions generate the best conversion rates.

EXAMPLES OF SUCCESSFUL OPTIMIZATION

- **Landing pages for specific services:** Create dedicated landing pages for different accounting services, each with specific messages and CTAs aimed at the corresponding target audience.

- **Simplified navigation bar:** Reduce clutter in your navigation bar to focus on links that direct visitors to the most important actions you want them to take.

- **Clear value offerings:** Ensure the value of your services is immediately clear to visitors by using persuasive copy that highlights the unique benefits you offer.

CHALLENGES IN CONVERSION OPTIMIZATION

- **Finding the right balance:** Too many calls to action or information can overwhelm visitors, while too little may not encourage them enough to take action.

- **Constant change:** User behavior and web design trends are always changing, requiring accountants to stay current and ready to adapt their websites as needed.

Equipped with strategies to optimize your website for conversion, the next step is to be inspired by successful cases in digital marketing for accountants.

In the next chapter, "**TARGETED CONTENT STRATEGIES**," we'll dive into how to create and distribute content that specifically resonates with each segment of your audience, maximizing engagement and conversion. Ready to customize your approach and achieve even better results? Let's proceed.

TARGETED CONTENT STRATEGIES

To maximize the impact of your digital marketing, it is crucial to adopt segmented content strategies. This means creating and distributing personalized content that addresses the specific needs, interests, and stages of the customer journey of different segments of your target audience. This approach not only increases relevance and engagement, but also conversion effectiveness. In this chapter, we'll explore how you can implement effective targeted content strategies for your accounting audience.

UNDERSTANDING CONTENT SEGMENTATION

Content segmentation involves dividing your target audience into smaller groups, or segments, based on specific criteria, such as industry, company size, accounting needs, position in the customer journey, among others. This allows you to customize your content to speak directly to each group's concerns and interests.

IMPLEMENTING SEGMENTED CONTENT STRATEGIES

- **Identify your audience segments:** Analyze your customer base and identify common patterns or categories that can be used to segment your audience. This may include new entrepreneurs, small businesses, technology startups, etc.

- **Develop customer personas:** For each identified segment, create detailed personas that represent typical customers within that group. Include your needs, challenges, goals and preferences.

- **Create personalized content:** Develop content that specifically addresses the interests and needs of each segment. For example, an e-book on "Financial Management for Startups" for technology entrepreneurs or a webinar on "Tax Reduction Strategies for Freelancers".

- **Choose the right channels:** Depending on the segment, some marketing channels may be more effective than others.

Identify where each segment of your audience spends the most time online and distribute your content across those channels.

- **Measure and adjust:** Use analytical tools to monitor the performance of your targeted content. Analyze engagement, conversions, and feedback to adjust your strategies as needed.

BENEFITS OF SEGMENTED CONTENT

- **Greater relevance:** Segmented content is perceived as more relevant by your audience, increasing engagement and the likelihood of conversion.

- **Strengthened relationships:** By demonstrating understanding of your customers' specific needs, you strengthen your relationship with them.

- **Cost efficiency:** Focusing your marketing efforts on the channels and messages that resonate with each segment can lead to a higher ROI by optimizing the use of your resources.

CHALLENGES OF SEGMENTED CONTENT

- **Complexity in execution:** Developing and managing multiple lines of content for different segments can be complex and require additional resources.

- **Segment identification:** Determining the most effective segments and their unique characteristics requires continuous research and analysis.

- **Maintaining brand consistency:** Ensuring that segmented content still reflects your brand's voice and values can be challenging when you're personalizing messages for diverse audiences.

Now that you understand how to create and implement targeted content strategies, the next step is to integrate customer feedback into the process. In the next chapter, " **CUSTOMER FEEDBACK**," we'll explore how to use customer reviews, comments, and behavior data to refine and optimize your targeted content strategies. Ready to close the feedback loop and continually improve your digital marketing? Let's move on.

CUSTOMER FEEDBACK

Integrating customer feedback into your digital marketing strategies is critical for continuous improvement and long-term success. This chapter focuses on how to collect, analyze, and use customer feedback to refine your targeted content strategies and other marketing initiatives. By better understanding your audience's needs and responses, you can adjust your approach to better serve your customers and optimize the effectiveness of your campaigns.

COLLECTING CUSTOMER FEEDBACK

- **Surveys and questionnaires:** Send email surveys after significant interactions, such as closing a service or attending a webinar, to gather insights into the customer experience.

- **Comments on social media:** Monitor social media to capture customer feedback and comments about your services or shared content.

- **Service reviews:** Encourage customers to leave reviews about your services on platforms like Google My Business and LinkedIn.

- **Direct feedback:** In direct conversations with customers, whether through virtual meetings or phone calls, take the opportunity to ask about their experiences and suggestions for improvements.

ANALYZING FEEDBACK

- **Identify trends:** Look for patterns in feedback that indicate areas of success or opportunities for improvement.

- **Prioritize feedback:** Not all feedback will require action, but it's important to identify which comments represent the needs of the majority of your customers.

- **Integration with content strategies:** Use feedback to inform the creation of segmented content, ensuring it resonates even more with different segments of your audience.

USING FEEDBACK FOR IMPROVEMENT

- **Content adjustment:** Refine your materials and messaging based on expressed needs and customer feedback to increase relevance and effectiveness.

- **Service improvements:** In addition to content, consider how feedback can help improve the services offered, from initial consultation to final delivery.

- **Development of new services:** Customer feedback can reveal opportunities for new services or products that meet emerging demands.

CHALLENGES IN USING FEEDBACK

- **Volume of feedback:** Managing and analyzing a large volume of feedback can be challenging, requiring effective data collection and analysis systems.

- **Contradictory feedback:** Sometimes you may receive conflicting feedback, making it difficult to decide which direction to go. In these cases, it's helpful to consider the feedback in the context of your broader business goals.

With a robust strategy for collecting and applying customer feedback in place, the next step is to look to the future. In the next chapter, "**FUTURE OF DIGITAL MARKETING IN ACCOUNTING**," we'll explore emerging trends and how you can prepare your accounting practice to adapt and thrive in the face of changes in the digital landscape. Ready to anticipate the future and maintain your competitive advantage? Let's move forward.

FUTURE OF DIGITAL MARKETING IN ACCOUNTING

As the digital world evolves, digital marketing in accounting continues to face rapid and significant changes. Anticipating these trends and adapting to them is crucial to maintaining competitiveness and seizing new opportunities. This chapter focuses on identifying emerging trends in digital marketing for accountants and how to prepare your accounting practice to thrive in the future.

EMERGING TRENDS IN ACCOUNTING DIGITAL MARKETING

- **Artificial intelligence and machine learning:** These technologies are becoming increasingly important for personalizing the customer experience and optimizing digital marketing campaigns. Tools that automate customer segmentation and personalize content based on user behavior will be essential.

- **Voice Marketing:** With the increased use of voice assistants, optimizing your content for voice search will become a necessity, adapting keywords and content to align with spoken queries.

- **Video marketing:** The preference for video content continues to grow. Short videos, interactive webinars and personalized video conferences will be key tools for engaging customers and prospects.

- **Data privacy and compliance:** With growing concerns about data privacy and the implementation of regulations like GDPR, demonstrating transparency and compliance in your digital marketing strategies will be even more critical.

- **Omnichannel marketing:** Integrating multiple platforms and channels to offer a cohesive customer experience, from social media to emails and websites, will be key to reaching the public effectively.

PREPARING FOR THE FUTURE

- **Continuing education:** Stay up to date on the latest tools, technologies and best practices in digital marketing by participating in webinars, conferences and courses.

- **Investment in technology:** Evaluate and invest in tools and platforms that allow the implementation of advanced marketing strategies, such as marketing automation, data analysis and personalization.

- **Strategic partnerships:** Consider partnering with digital marketing and technology experts to expand your capabilities and innovate your strategies.

- **Customer focus:** Continue to put customer needs and preferences at the center of your marketing planning, adapting to changes in consumer behavior and expectations.

ANTICIPATED CHALLENGES

- **Adapting to technological changes:** Staying ahead in adopting new technologies can be challenging due to the rapid pace of innovation.

- **Balancing automation and personalization:** Finding the right balance between efficiency and personalization continues to be a challenge as more processes are automated.

Now that we've explored the future trends of digital marketing in accounting, the next step is to ensure you're on the right track. In the next chapter, **"DIGITAL MARKETING CHECKLIST FOR ACCOUNTANTS"**, we will provide a comprehensive list to help you evaluate and optimize your current digital marketing strategy. This tool will be essential in ensuring you are making the most of your digital marketing initiatives. Ready to review and revitalize your digital marketing strategy? Let's move forward.

DIGITAL MARKETING CHECKLIST FOR ACCOUNTANTS

To ensure your digital marketing strategy is aligned with best practices and prepared to capture opportunities, it's important to regularly review your activities and plans. This chapter offers a comprehensive checklist for accountants and accounting professionals to review and optimize their digital marketing strategy.

DIGITAL MARKETING CHECKLIST

1 - OPTIMIZED WEBSITE:

- Responsive design for mobile devices.

- Fast loading speed.

- Updated and relevant content.

- Clear and visible calls to action.

2 - SEO (SEARCH ENGINE OPTIMIZATION):

- Keywords relevant to your target audience.

- SEO-optimized content, including titles, meta descriptions, and alt tags on images.

- Link building strategy to improve domain authority.

3 - CONTENT MARKETING:

- Editorial calendar for blogs, videos and other content.

- Segmented content based on customer personas.

- Use of storytelling to make content more engaging.

4 - PRESENCE ON SOCIAL MEDIA:

- Updated and active profiles on platforms relevant to your audience.

- Plan for regular posts and engagement with the public.

- Monitoring brand mentions and quickly responding to comments or questions.

5 – EMAIL MARKETING:

- Segmented email list based on interest or stage in the customer journey.

- Automation campaigns to nurture leads.

- Regular analysis of performance metrics such as open and click rates.

6 - ONLINE ADS:

- Well-targeted PPC (pay per click) campaigns on Google Ads or social platforms.

- Analysis and continuous adjustment of campaigns based on performance.

- A/B testing of ads to optimize conversions.

7 - ANALYSIS AND METRICS:

- Use of Google Analytics to monitor traffic, sources and behavior on the website.

- Analysis of the ROI of different marketing channels and campaigns.

- Strategic adjustments based on data insights.

8 - FEEDBACK AND ADAPTATION:

- Regular collection of customer feedback through surveys or analysis of online interactions.

- Adaptation of the marketing strategy based on feedback and market trends.

9 - COMPLIANCE AND DIGITAL ETHICS:

- Regular review of privacy policies and compliance with regulations such as GDPR.

- Guarantee that all marketing practices respect ethical principles.

This checklist serves as a guide to keeping your digital marketing strategy aligned with best practices and adapted to the evolving needs of your target audience. Regularly reviewing and optimizing these elements will ensure your marketing initiatives are effective and efficient, helping you achieve your business objectives.

After reviewing and adjusting your strategy based on the checklist, the next step is to implement the necessary changes. In the next chapter, "**30 DAY ACTION PLAN**", we will outline a step-by-step guide to putting your revitalized digital marketing strategy into practice, ensuring a quick and effective start to see real results. Ready to take the next steps and transform your accounting practice? Let's move on.

30 DAY ACTION PLAN

After refining your digital marketing strategy based on the comprehensive checklist, it's time to put these improvements into practice. A 30-day action plan can be extremely effective in initiating significant change, allowing you to see tangible results in a short period of time. This chapter offers a step-by-step guide to implementing the necessary updates and optimizations in your digital marketing strategy.

WEEK 1: ASSESSMENT AND PLANNING

- **Day 1-2:** Conduct a full audit of your current website and social media presence to identify areas that need immediate improvement.

- **Day 3-4:** Set clear goals for what you want to achieve with your digital marketing strategy in the next 30 days. These goals should be specific, measurable, achievable, relevant, and time-bound (SMART).

- **Day 5-7:** Create a content calendar for your website blog, marketing emails, and social media posts for the next 30 days.

WEEK 2: IMPLEMENTATION AND OPTIMIZATION

- **Day 8-10:** Update your website design and content to ensure it is responsive, fast and SEO optimized.

- **Day 11-14:** Start producing and publishing planned content. This includes writing blog posts, preparing marketing emails and creating social media posts.

WEEK 3: PROMOTION AND ENGAGEMENT

- **Day 15-17:** Set up or optimize your online ad campaigns, including Google Ads and ads on social media platforms, focusing on your key audience segments.

- **Day 18-21:** Increase engagement on social media by interacting with followers, responding to comments and participating in relevant conversations.

WEEK 4: ANALYSIS AND ADJUSTMENT

- **Day 22-24:** Use analytical tools to review the performance of published content, ad campaigns, and social media engagement. Identify what is working well and what needs to be adjusted.

- **Day 25-27:** Make adjustments to strategies based on analysis, whether it's modifying content, pausing underperforming ad campaigns, or reinforcing ones that are working well.

- **Day 28-30:** Plan the next month based on the insights gained, adjusting your content calendar and marketing strategies as needed.

This 30-day action plan is a starting point for putting your improved digital marketing strategy into motion. The key to continued success is the ability to iterate quickly - utilizing feedback, analytics and market trends to inform future decisions and continually optimize your marketing approach.

By following this plan, you will establish a solid foundation for your digital marketing initiatives, creating momentum for future growth and continued refinement of your strategies. Remember, digital marketing is a dynamic process; Being willing to adapt and innovate is key to achieving and maintaining long-term success.

As we turn the final page of this journey together, I sincerely hope that the learnings shared here have touched your heart and sparked new perspectives. If this book has brought you any value, I kindly ask that you take a few moments to leave a review on Amazon. Your words not only help me grow and hone my craft, but they also guide other readers in their quests for knowledge and inspiration. Your opinion is a valuable gift, both for me and for the community of readers looking for stories that transform. I sincerely thank you for sharing this journey with me and I hope we can meet again in the pages of a new adventure.

REGINALDO OSNILDO

Hello, I'm Reginaldo Osnildo, author and innovator in the fields of sales, technology, and communication strategies. My background spans from the academic setting, as a professor and researcher at the University of Southern Santa Catarina, to hands-on strategy development at the Catarinense Radio Group. With a PhD in sales narratives and digital convergence, and a Master's in storytelling and social imaginary, I offer my readers a unique blend of theory and practice. My aim is to deliver knowledge in a simple, practical, and didactic language, encouraging direct application in one's personal and professional life.

Yours sincerely

Reginaldo Osnildo

+55 48 991913865

reginaldoosnildo@gmail.com